Long Island Haunts

An Anthology of Poems & Stories

Edited by
James P. Wagner (Ishwa)

Long Island Haunts

Table of Contents

William Aiello

Is There Anything You Fear?

Jason and Lori were dating, for about a year
When Jason asked Lori, "Is there anything you fear?"

She responded quite promptly, "What I fear the most"
She paused, then she finished, "It's surely a ghost"

Jason then said, "The reason I asked
There was something outdoors, appeared to be masked"

Lori was puzzled, but Jason replied
"It looked like a ghost, and it was outside"

"Oh stop it, you nut, don't try to be sly
You know, and I know, it's purely a lie"

But the party tonight, was drawing quite near
The company was coming, and they'd soon be there

Jason was off to pick up the cherry crumb cake
And Lori was finishing the fruit salad she'd make

She heard the car start, and he hit the road
It got awfully quiet, you could hear a toad

The wind, it was rushing, much more than a breeze
The leaves they were flying, and swaying of trees

Lori opened the door, there were sounds like a boo
She looked left and right, she heard howling, too

Lori went inside, maybe just strong wind
The cat was asleep, the dog hadn't spinned

But now these strange sounds were heard in the celler
She got much alarmed, is there maybe some feller?

She checked downstairs, no one to be seen
The dog hadn't barked, no one was fleein'

Back to her work, and what did she see?
A ghost at the table, sitting quietly

She screamed and she hollered, "My word, there's a ghost!"
But the spirit assured her, "Do not fear, my host"

"What are you here for, what do you want?"
The ghost smiled and answered, "I'm not here to haunt"

"There's just one reason, one thing I must take
Will you please give me a slice of the cherry crumb cake?"

William "Bill" is a writer, actor, ventriloquist, poet. He has had three books published, the most recent this past week. Also a short story, numerous poems. He appeared in an episode of "Billions" earlier this year. Bill is co-Executive Director of a local preliminary to the Miss New York and Miss Americas titles. His ventriloquism routines can be seen at an open mike event monthly or online at Facebook or YouTube.

Patricia Z. Beach

The Manor

She stands on top of Fort Hill bluff.
Overlooking the beach front and sea with vistas of
The Atlantic Ocean, Gardiners Bay and Long Island Sound.
This land once belonged to native tribes.
They gathered at Council Rock and buried their dead.
The Manor rests on land of bloody conflict
The Montaukett tribe was slaughtered
By the New England Narragansetts nearby.
Centuries later during the Roaring Twenties
Carl Fisher erected a Tudor-style hotel upon this site.
Flappers and Gatsby-like squires
Partied over the bones of these brave warriors.
The stock market crash stopped the dancing.
The Manor fell into disrepair.
The castle was abandoned and stood empty.
Only its turrets and spires
Kept watch over these Long Island waters.
Years later it was restored to its former glory
Including its cavernous lobby and vaulted 18-foot ceilings.
Some say Montauk Manor is haunted.
Guests have seen a proud Native American Chief
His restless spirit roams the halls and corridors.
They hear drumbeats, doors slammed and chanting.
Others prefer to ignore any talk of spirit intervention.
For today Montauk and the Manor are luxury destinations.

Patricia Z. Beach is pursuing her passion for writing after a diverse career in transportation management. Publications include PPA Literary Review (vol. 21), Bards Annual years 2016, 2021 and Chicken Soup for the Soul (2019). A recipient of Long Island Literary Arts prose award (2019 2nd place), Patricia holds a BA in English from St. John's University and a MS in Construction Management from NYU. She is a member of the Farmingdale Creative Writing Group.

Maureen Blesi

The Search

Follow me down to the bottom deep
it is here where I treasure the souls that I reap.
None can ever replace my one true love
for he is long gone on the wings of a dove.
Heartbeat pulses with an intense desire
as I lure young men into the depths of muck and mire.
A collection of souls to keep me company
in our watery grave we float eternally.

Our quilt of silt, our watery bed
cradles all those who are truly dead.
We share the depths of this lovely lake
I, awaiting another soul to take.
Perhaps I shall never find another Hugh,
but I continue to create my human stew.
Thus, you should think twice before you wade in
for it may turn out to be your last swim.

Do not lament if they are not found
for tis' certain they have most likely drown.
Peaceful amongst the centuries of souls
who entered the lake and paid the toll.
None can replace my beloved Hugh

though each year I try to find someone new.
In life, an Indian Princess I had been
but in death my seductive powers are without end.

Be wary, do not even dip in your hand,
nor sit on the edge of the brown, wet sand.
Never go swimming alone in the night,
not even in daytime when the sun shines bright.
For I have reign over this beautiful lake
and what I want is what I shall take.
So heed the warnings form those who tell
of the haunted lake where the Princess dwells.

Maureen Blesi, - Amateur poet.

Maggie Bloomfield

On the Way to the Halloween Party

The monsters roll

They zoom, crawl, hover, swerve.
Irritating every nerve.

The monsters roll

Gothlike colors flash ahead,
Black or, silver, orange red,
Cats" eyes flash to leave you blind
Racing toward you or behind.
Apple rounds of LED
Guarantee you can not see.

The monsters roll

Escalades and rams that crush
others in their tortured rush
toward a party planned in Hell
Will this Halloween end well?

Murky creatures lurk within,
Corpse of bride and ghosts who grin.
Skeletons thrust bony wrists
Tatted bikers shake their fists.

If you 're lucky and survive,
Comes the drunken homeward drive.
Bats and cats and witches reign,
It's the LIE... again..

Maggie Bloomfield is a psychotherapist, published poet/essayist, per-
former, Emmy-winning lyricist for Sesame Street. Two chap-
books: *Trains of Thought,* published by Local Gems, 2017, and
S*leepless Nights*, Finishing Line Press, 2020. Plays include, *BREAK
OUT!* written and performed with Susan Dingle, East End
Fringe Festival, 2017, and *The Dispatchment Society,* chosen for
NYC New Works Emerging Artist Festival, 2019. Maggie co-hosts
Poetry Street, a hybrid monthly poetry venue at The Riverhead Li-
brary and on ZOOM.
www.maggiebloomfield.com

Philip Buttafuoco

Asylum

It was a weary, dark, creepy, lonely night
Lost and stranded
A desolate road
Rusty fence with torn down gate
Overgrown weeds slamming my car
Buildings a far
Dark, abandoned, in disarray

The headlights were slowly........ dimming
My heart, throbbing
My thoughts, rampant
My eyes dashing
Prayed to the patron saint
What's out there?
Should I go out?

My machoness exulted my fear
Out I went
Needles pinching my leg
Distant voices,
Screaming! Crying! Moaning!
I was trembling
The voices were daunting
My leg expunged a thorny branch
Where am I?

I walked slowly, lack of visibility
I heard crackling as I fell
Tumbling down a hill
I saw visions of the afterlife
I touched fury something
Wet and sticky
My eyes straining to move
Restrained by my fear
A lopsided wooden sign above me
Kings Park Psychiatric Center

Born in Sicily Italy. He immigrated to America in 1962. Phil served in the US Air Force as a technician on Fighter-Jets. Through his vast experiences, he began writing poems and short stories. In 1981 while in college he had 5 poems published in the "VOICES Literary Magazine" published by Suny College at Old Westbury NY. He recently self-published a children's picture book, titled "Andre Learning Hair Styling."

Samantha Curra

The Black Chandelier

In her quarters she rests, dear beloved Camille
Preserved and kept in solitary time
The latent dust never rises, settled still
In her silent asylum she lies

She dreams of dancing under darkened skies
Where the moonlight adorns the dead
If she still had lids she would open her eyes
As he sits at the foot of her bed

He cradles the corpse with a temperate lift
So not to puncture her porcelain sphere
Into the ballroom the candles are lit
As they dance under the black chandelier

With her feet off the ground she moves with his pace
Until the dawn exposes the day
You can almost remember the smile on her face
Before the skin slowly rotted away

Patient Camille, all she has is time
She waits for him to appear
She may be dead but she feels most alive
Underneath the black chandelier

Samantha Curra is a dog-loving, coffee-fueled poet and copywriter. Her literary work has been featured in multiple publications, including *Bards Annual*; *Narrateur*, *Reflections on Caring;* and *Prompt Literary Magazine*, among others. A fanatic for word games, she enjoys playing Wordle and has yet to be defeated in Boggle.

India DeCarmine

Boney Lane

Say you're out walking down Boney Lane,
in your Nike Airs, with your wolf's head cane.
It's midnight, or past, but the midnight air
is cleansing. And you don't easily scare.

Though -
you've heard of a man who never came back,
one night while treading this very track.
One night, in a century not your own,
Old Willet walked out, and never came home.

But that is a story from ages ago.
Perhaps it's true. Hell, you'll never know.
Meantime, the cane stays tight in your grip,
and your cellphone's a comfort, there on your hip.
There are but trees, and darkness, near.
Nothing a modern man needs to fear.

Say you're out walking down Boney Lane,
when you hear a voice that doesn't sound sane
-whispering, carried along by the breeze,
coming from somewhere off in the trees-
desperate and ragged and chillingly pitched,
the voice of some poor devil bewitched.

14

Let's think. Do you merely quicken your pace,
or does a modern man choose to race
faster and in the direction of home?
And in his haste does he notice his phone
buzzing and buzzing, like some toy alarm,
useless, but signaling proximate harm?

Say you're now running down Boney Lane,
in your Nike Airs, with your wolf's head cane,
Running, as if your life now depended
on dodging the demon Old Willet befriended,
that night in a century not your own,
when a man walked out and never came home.
An old fireside tale from ages ago;
You doubted it once.
HELL.
Now you know.

Say they go searching, down Boney Lane.
They find just your phone, and Old Willet's cane.

India DeCarmine loves to walk in the woods. From her wonderful
mother, she learned to love both nature and all things haunted.
Thus, if the woods are haunted, so much the better. India lives, and
walks, on Long Island.

Ben Diamond

The Magnificent Frigate

The male frigate is
the most advanced independent flying
creature of our world, for
he possesses the greatest wing
surface to body weight
ratio of any bird. He can
soar for hours high above
the sea without a single flap of wings,
He can eat, drink, preen,
and even sleep while flying.

He wears a bold-face
"M" across his chest to signify
"Magnificent,"
his gleaming wings and body
form a great black cape.
He cannot fish below the surface,
for he may not wet his wings,
and in order to survive
has turned to piracy.

In February
a sack of tissue by his throat
turns pinkish-red like scrotum skin.

He then inflates the sack
into a big bright-red balloon.
All this he does while
perching in the low lands to appeal
to females overhead, like the teens
in Levittown who stand beside
the open hoods of muscle cars,
attracting high-haired girls.

Born, raised, and still living in East Meadow, NY, Ben Diamond is a songwriter and new age beat poet. Like Charles Baudelaire, Ben writes songs and poems that are quintessentially useless and absolutely innocent, and written with no other aim than to divert himself and to practice his passionate taste for the difficult.

Valerie Griggs

Oak Beach Inn

We rode the first wind to Island Park,
OBI West, our favorite haunt.
On the second wind, we danced to
OBI South, Jones Beach,
the third we sailed to Hampton Bays,
OBI East. We never made it north.

Ladies' night, blinking lights,
live music, flies in ice cubes,
bikers, boaters, plastic cups,
barroom brothers, jokers,
smokers. Symbols of the
parting of ways, our days.

Bye-bye Mr. 60s haze, maze
self-important druggy craze.
We knew who was lying,
and it wasn't our parents;
we knew who was trying,
and it wasn't politicians.

We built stairways, brick roads,
bridges over troubled causes,
our earth shoes, Marshmallow
sole shoes skipping away from

mythical guardians, childhood
dependance. We were alive

and kicking in those haunts,
fake IDs not confusing us.

We taught each other in
the streets, the open roads,
on the beach, rollin' us down
the highway until we were ready

to survive, be scattered
over gritty New York City,
imbibe liquid courage
and step into alma maters
dotting the American landscape.
Stale beer, cigarette fug, dares,

tiny dancers singing, laughing.
Bouncers knew our names; the bands,
the mean girls, the creepy guys,
buy-backs, the dark, the wood –
it must've been the ocean,
it must've been the bay,

it must've been the ennui
that called us to grow up,
take a chance, ramble on,
fly, come sail away into time
ticking into the future. Nothing
clings like those old haunts.

Born in Brooklyn and a new resident of Suffolk County, Valerie Griggs has been writing poetry, fiction, essays and songs for over 30 years. She won first prize in the 2023 Nassau County Poet Laureate Society's poetry contest. Her work has appeared in over a dozen literary journals and magazines.

Daryel Groom

Rapunzel's Lighthouse

In 1811 a Christmas evening storm shipwrecked young Abigail upon
Montauk Point Lighthouse shores
last light drowned by relentless winter tempest battling her for last
tired breath
rescued only to diminish inside the refuge of the lighthouse walls
centuries later cold breezes soft murmurs in empty silence furniture
moving slight touches by your ghostly grace many have testified
flickering through the halls and stairways
awaiting a love forbidden by your father's vow
a lover who worked at the lighthouse 212 years ago
have you harbored in search of him
speaking in echoes shapeshifting castle of lost light lost love
lingering specter do you cross paths with ghosts familiar
Walt Whitman George Washington Teddy Roosevelt or British Sol-
diers surveying the Turtle Hill
lurking misty fog mimicking shores you harbor as a relic of time sus-
pended
forever 17 in your seaside castle settled in the memory of treasures
shipwrecks
pirates sea creatures abound
Rapunzel of the lighthouse tower
illuminate your guiding light on mariners facing tumultuous seas
against our mighty point

Heidi C. Hallett

Haunted Home

Stately, old, Victorian home,
lakeside, cedar shake and stone.
Noble host to formal soirées
with silver and porcelain back in the day.
Private balls no longer in fashion,
seen as vintage passion, a fine horse and sleigh.

Nowadays, local legend has it,
on eves late and starred,
you can still hear satin strains
of shining, ballroom music
with footsteps twirling
on classic, dance hall parquet.

Stately, old, Victorian home,
spirit held within her stone.

Haunted to remind
of future dreams denied?
Haunted to hang on
to living-love bond?
Or haunted as a Gilded Age sign
of a portal in time?

Stately, old, Victorian home,
cedar shake and stone unknown.

Heidi C. Hallett sees creative expression through poetry as a way to collaborate and converse. She finds that poetry enables us to examine and appreciate life, and she enjoys working with the imagery in poems to explore ideas. Heidi is a recently retired, small animal veterinarian who paints with oils as well as words, often using these two art forms to complement each other. She is the author of several poetry chapbooks through Local Gems Press, and her poetry has been published in on-line and print journals as well as in numerous print anthologies. www.aquaartideas.com.

Rowan K

Abandoned Buildings

Abandoned buildings call me home like a beacon in the night. To some they are old buildings. Standing empty, alone, and broken. In desperate need of being torn down and rebuilt in a style to match the times, and with a purpose to fit a need.
But they are wrong.

Abandoned buildings stand as a symbol of resistance, hope, and proof
that 2 opposites can co-exist peacefully within one shell. These abandoned buildings call me.
Personifying my fear of being left alone to rot, forgotten by the progressing times.

But they also hold a unique beauty,
standing tall and proud against an uncertain future.

Fee from the labels of its past.
Waiting to make a new name.

Forgiven by some.
Forgotten by others,
Untold by many.

These buildings stand:

Whole and empty;
free and chained;
loud and silent;
full of a pain promising a brighter future.

These buildings stand abandoned, yet unforgotten by those who know how to see beyond what meets the eye.

These buildings leave me with a feeling of serenity.
Giving me the strength to continue building a home within my broken walls.
Because abandoned does not mean alone, forgotten, and unwanted; but rather stands to represent the delicate balance of negative and positive that is needed to stand tall, unmoved, and beautiful in a world that would rather move on than move forward.

Rowan is a 25 year old poet. She currently attends Adelphi University pursuing a Masters in General Psychology. She recently published her first poetry book entitled, "Trauma." She also has poems published in the US, UK, and India.

Edward Kenny

Beware Of The Scarecrow

So, you've had enough of my idle threats,
Think it's just big talk from someone small,
Those ill-chosen words that you forced me to say,
While my back was pressed to the wall.

The crows have a mind to pick the fields clean,
'Til the dark foreboding figure of me
Hastens their retreat, but soon,
They're inching closer and closer to me,'

In a bold moment,
They decide to peck my rags away,
Just to feel me out,
And see if I'm really stuffed with hay,
Beware of the scarecrow,
There's only so much pecking he can take
Don't pull his patient seams
Until they break.

This scarecrow doesn't dance to snapping fingers,
And he won't fight over things you say,
He doesn't post notice of his boundaries,
But he protects his fields anyway.

And a quiet sentry is a joke
To the crows that think an iron hand
Is the only proof that
A peaceful figure can still be a man.

In a bold moment,
They decide to peck my rags away,
Just to feel me out,
And see if I'm really stuffed with hay,
Beware of the scarecrow,
There's only so much pecking he can take
Don't pull his patient seams
Until they break.

Edward Kenny is an author, lyricist and librettist. He has published
several books of poetry and lyrics, including two verse plays/librettos.
He has written the book and lyrics for 11 musicals, including one
that was selected as a finalist in the New York Drama League's
Grants Competition, along with over 1,400 lyrics.

Denise Kolanovic

When the Squire Comes

For Adrienne and John

You steal them from us.
You, the abysmal squire who takes away
Our kings and queens,
Tearing our hearts with your fangs and poison daggers
Ripping into softness, once protected
By perfect unicorn dreams.
You are the second guesser of strange
Circumstances that strip
Our inner voice, a flame,
So that dull droning sounds escape
And we, entrapped in fearful contemplation
And isolated rage scratch our skin against cement.
We scream the dreadful cries of Antigone
Who drags again her brother's bloody body from the vultures.
We taste the sour metal flavor of blood
For we have gnawed our tongues in curses to you.
You wretched power,
Go to your world of currents, of whirlpools
That roam the earth. Go!
You open shadow doors to our blurred vision
And we must gain composure from your fission
Of madness and disparity.

When wondering reddens all thought
And unwelcome devils gloat
In our despair, we sit silently
Waiting for the semblance of pure snow.
And in the whitening moment of eye blink
The colors become clearer and the center stage
Is set again of new vintages and soothing rain.

Denise Kolanovic is an English/ENL teacher and a poet. She has been published in *Whispers and Shouts, Reckless Writing, Long Island Quarterly, Walt's Corner, Celiyd, Bards Anthologies, PPA Anthologies,* and others. She co-edited *Eve's Legacy* and authored *Asphalt Sounds,* Fore Angels Press: 2004 and *Magnetized by Black Irises,* Words With Wings: 2020.

Iris Levin

haunting images

what I saw
what I didn't see
on the front page
years ago

I saw a soldier
lifting a child's body out of the water
gently carrying him to his burial

I saw that child washed ashore
still wearing -- red t-shirt, black shorts, little black sneakers
his eyes closed
his arms at his sides
as if asleep
as if dreaming
of a better tomorrow

I didn't see his fear
as the boat overturned
as he slipped from mother's embrace
as she floated away
washed up on a different shore

and today

different haunting images
but the same headline

HUMAN TRAGEDY

Iris Levin writes with open heart and open eyes. An observational poet,she sees her work as snapshots of life, short probing images..She has been published in on line and printed anthologies.

Steve Levy

The Zombie House

The house across the street from us
Has been vacant for 5 years
A zombie house
Too many liens against it, too out of code, too dilapidated and too
expensive to fix up
The house sits vacant for 7 years or so until all is forgiven, and
some adventurous investor comes in to flip it for a nice little profit
5 long years it sits vacant, overgrown with shrubs and grime, just
waiting to come back to life.

So imagine our surprise when a dumpster appears in the driveway.
Workers are clearing it out
A car pulls up, and a friendly couple comes out to greet us

"Hi, we're your new neighbors! Nice to meet you, I'm Ronnie, and
this is Viv"
We shake hands and exchange pleasantries
So nice to have new neighbors… got any kids… where you from, we
didn't even know the house was on the market.
"Yeah, we got lucky, got it as a short sale"
"Well congratulations. Anything you need, just let us know."

Another neighbor was pissed, and chewed out his realtor
She was supposed to keep an eye out for that property for when it
became available.
But I have been, she replied
Well, then how come these new people just moved in?

What? she said in astonishment. That can't be, I'm looking at the report right here, not for sale
Well, they already got the dumpster, and they're clearing out the house.
They're squatters, they're illegally occupying that house. Call the police.

But our neighbor didn't want to get the police involved.
He gave them one chance.
Had his crew come up, confronted them, told them he knew they're little game, and that if they didn't get the hell out, he'd get the cops.

We never saw Ronnie and Viv again.
Our neighbor said that had they established residence, even illegally for 30 days, they could claim squatters rights
We were always warned about squatters in that house
Thought they'd be homeless, vagrant looking.
Never imagined a bunch of con-artists,
An affluent looking pair
But in the game of keeping up with the Joneses,
Make sure to know who you're really keeping up with

Steve Levy is blessed to have two wonderful children, Dylan and Mackenzie and a loving and supportive wife Kelly, who put up with all his dad jokes. A teacher by day, jack of all trades by night, he still works on that illusive first novel or poetry collection, whenever the muse visits him, as sparingly as that is.

Gene McParland

Reverse Trick or Treat

Ring! Ring! Ring!
There goes the doorbell again.
It's Halloween!
It's a perfect Autumn Fall day;
a super day for trick or treating,
and all the little monster
are out and about.

3 bags with that bunch.
Wow! a couple of dozen bags, so far.
A real busy Halloween.
All the treats are bagged and sealed,
important to do
 during these still COVID times.

I know that one of those
little costumed kiddies.
will be getting a real surprise
when he or she opens her bag.

I got to say I'm not even sure
which bag I put the big surprise in
any more. It's a very valuable
diamond ring.

I know I paid a fortune for it
a dozen years ago, when
I brought it for my (unfaithful) wife.

She doesn't need it any more,
and I certainly don't want it.
So why not make it
a very memorable Halloween surprise.

The only problem is
the lucky winner
will still have to remove it
from my wife's finger.

As they say -
Trick or Treat!

Gene McParland (North Babylon, NY): is a graduate from Queens College and also possesses graduate degrees from other institutions. He has always had a passion for poetry and the message that it can convey. His poems have appeared in numerous poetry publications over the years. He is the author of <u>Baby Boomer Ramblings, a collection of essays and poetry.</u> He is also the author of, <u>Adult Without, Child Within</u>, a collection on poetry celebrating the child within all of us. He also acts in local theater and videos, and has written several plays.

CR Montoya

Music, Mirth, Memories

The place had a pull like an aurora,
you knew this visit would be an echo of the last
though it was human catnip, irresistible.

As you stepped inside, your senses were arrested
first, the floor vibrated with gyrating bodies,
the wash of color bouncing from a sea of Madras shirts.

Without a chance to orient,
a mix of aromas embraced you,
sun tan lotion, alcohol, and sweat.

The place had its own special vibe
college kids in beige slacks, colorful shirts, and tees,
white sneakers with a dash of mini-skirts.

Surfers and beach bunnies made up most of the throng,
They coordinated with the surfboard hanging over the bar.

Tunes of the Beach Boys resonated,
Little Surfer Girl, a favored song to ease the pace,
and create a dreamy mood.

Guys gaining consent from a pretty girl

brightened for the chance - a slow dance,
hoping for a back-to-back to create a memory.

If luck was on the menu, you'd start a conversation
anything to extend the moment, and hope for her number.

The weekend, the game,
a chance for summer fun.

The 60s, Main Street, Farmingdale, - PJs.

CR Montoya publishes children's stories, featuring *Papa The Happy Snowman*. He published a short story titled *Return to Bedford Falls* in January 2022. Based on the movie *It's A Wonderful Life*, the story carries readers through time describing how the lives of the movies glorious characters evolved after that fateful Christmas Eve. His latest work is titled, *Sophie's Unicorn, A Tale of Wonder. Sophie's Unicorn is a delightful, lighthearted children's story sprinkled with caring, love, and humor. These works can be found on Amazon. His poetry can be found in various Long Island anthologies, such as Nassau County Voices and the Bards publications.*

Mary Sheila Morrissey

Long Island Haunts

Long Island haunted me.
Nearly daily during decades of exile to California.
Recollections of a Kings Park-upbringing comforted
and tormented.
Plaid wool jumpers, beanies, white knee socks of
St. Joseph's School-last graduating class before it closed in '72.

The bowling machine and the myna bird in the Club House Tavern
on 25A—my parents were part-owners. A big German Shepard out
back had its throat cut once but survived.

The big Psych Center where my sister had been a patient
and later an employee.

My world slightly expanded to include Smithtown's hot, muggy
YMCA Day Camp summer days, bored and bullied,
only the days that included horseback riding
were tolerable.
Barely.

Senior year at KPHS—the most vivid and precious months.
Sense memories heightened.
Bagel runs during study hall to someplace down passed
Billy Blake's on Jericho—pumpernickel, please.

Carvel in a blizzard if a hot fudge sundae would brighten the mood
—such a crush on the boy from my class that worked there.

First date skating at Superior Ice Rink, falling down, laughing,
a good camouflage for our nervousness.

"Nashville" at the KP movie theatre, "The Omen" at the Commack
Drive-in.
Pizza Hut sangria and Ground Round peanut shelled linoleum.

A back seat parked on Echo Lane or Landing Avenue where child-
hood and
clothing were discarded and
choices made were often revisited and second guessed.
Long Island haunted me nearly every day I lived in California,
trying to ditch the accent, replace "pocketbook" with "purse"
–fit in.
Survived seasonless years, hot tubs on Christmas Day, "night and
mid-morning clouds—high of 73"
Octobers were the worst…or was it January?
My shell hardened in the Santa Ana howling winds,
numbed, I curled inward and pressed on,
never dreaming that I could return.

Older, wiser, bitter, battered
I travelled back for a nostalgic short visit one October
Just two days…that was all it took….
92692 became 11717

Long Island haunts me no more.

Mary Sheila Morrissey was raised in Kings Park. She has published five books of poetry and just completed her first novel. Mary has worked in academic libraries all her life and is blessed to have returned home to Long Island. She resides in Brentwood.

Susan O'Byrne

Halloween Jaunt

I always visit my favorite haunt
On October 31st when I'm wont to flaunt
My bona fide outfit
I can't live without it
I saunter about on a familiar jaunt
Past eerie homes with ghoulish front lawns
Decked out in ghastly Halloween décor
Tombstones, headstones covered in gore
In my heyday I knocked on each door
Said, "Trick or Treat!" for candy galore
Didn't go home until streetlights came on
Walked with friends with disguises on
But that is quite a long time gone
Now a costume I don't deign to don
I don't like to brag but I scare away
The bravest of men with one look my way
I frighten children on their mad candy dash
I startle apple dunkers at their Halloween bash
They cry out bemused, but somewhat enthused,
"A skeleton costume's a bit overused!"
To them my appearance is downright trite
But I'm part of the gang again to my delight
For I am a skeleton; gaunt, white and bony

Ossified, calcified, rickety, not phony
One day a year I walk among men
To feel like a flesh and blood human again

Susan O'Byrne is a Spanish, French and English as a New Language tutor for homebound students. She enjoys writing songs in all three languages to reinforce vocabulary lessons.

Greg Resnick

Dreams

What never was
is often that which unseen.
A lost one
wandering forever
the miasma
of the dark.

We search for answers
unseen but sort after.
A life of solitude
in a distant land
often dreamed of.

The children
dream one real.
That which is unreal
a second reflection
alter the destiny
of the masses.

Veering in the dark
can destroy the light.
Forever lost
in the nothingness.

43

Rita B. Rose

Cheating Death

The reaper was posting names in Grim Scrolls
He sat his blade in the dirt with a *clink*
Surnames were etched upon gray granite stone
And when mine was carved I let out a s*hriek*!

Inch by inch I neared the fixed reaping tool
My stoney stare on death personified
Glad a hoodie concealed this ghastly ghoul
As I seized his sickle with a hushed cry

We battled for many souls in twilight
under a crescent moon who blind his orbs
thus, swiftly I pilfered Death's steely scythe
and me and Moon howled 'til we could no more

For we had quelled death's unwelcoming knell
Life was prolonged for a brief winter's spell

Rita B. Rose is an internationally published poet and the current Long Island LGBTQ Poet Laureate she is also the recipient of two Bards awards and an LGBTQ + Lifetime Achievement Award

A. A. Rubin

The Widow's Walk (1849)

Cold Spring Harbor, 1849
I walk around the roof at night,
Up above my home—
Waiting for his ship to sight,
My husband to return—

The townsfolk they all think I'm mad,
"His ship's gone down," they say.
"Sunk she was, all lives were lost,
Buried 'neath the waves—"

But still I wend my way around,
The walk above my home—
Between the ocean and the moon,
A widow, now, alone—

For though I know his ship's been lost,
Sunk beneath the sea—
On certain nights, his ghost returns,
And keeps me company—

We sit and talk throughout the night,
Until the break of day—
When waves are crowned with dawn's first light,
And ghosts must fade away—

A. A. Rubin exists only in dreams within dreams. His gothic collection Into That Darkness Peering (illustrated by Marika Brousianou) was nominated for the Poe Visiter Award (Edgar Allan Poe House and Museum), and his poem "Night Walkers" won first place in the inaugural Poe-It-Like-Poe contest (The Six Degrees of Edgar Allan Poe). His poetry has appeared in Love Letters to Poe, The Deronda Review, and Poetica. He can be reached on social media as @TheSurrealAri, or through his website www.aarubin.com. A connoisseur of fine amontillado, he has been known to clean mysterious white stains off the bust of Pallas which sits on his writing desk. He loves with a love that is more than love.

Kaycee Ryan

A Song by the Sea

My mother, my mother had sang unto me
A song, a song at the edge of the sea
Lulled was I, by the breath of the reeds
To soon, to soon did the waves snatch with greed

Plucked from my nest before I could fly
The sound of my cry still piercing the sky
Weathering the heights of a faraway land
Falling up, climbing down - I'm tumbling down

They clung on to me, like the salt of the sea
His talons are whispers, digging softly in me
On strings I now fly, it's a sweet lullaby
Oh to where, to where- I'm going nowhere

Lost in the dark, only fools to be crowned
All I've found, run aground- I wander around

But the sea, my sea- It still calls out to me
As I'm burning my fingers on dear memories

But the sea, our sea- It still calls out for me
Where the branches still sway, in a keep by the bay

47

Away, away- on a cliff far away
Where the mist of the tides still keep her alive
Alone, alone- she wanders alone
Where the dogmatic lessons of liar's be sown

The harbor, the harbor now sings unto me
The tale, the tale of a withered oak tree
To yonder it drifts, on a river of night
Like a ship, oh a ship that sets sail at first light

Her phantom, her phantom still sings unto me
A song, a song at the edge of the sea
Enraptured am I, with the full lunar's might
To the rhythm, the rhythm of the stars I now write

Kaycee is a 26 year old Long Island native who's been writing stories since she learned to hold a pencil. When not working on her novel, she often spends her spare time drawing, studying foreign languages and trying not to be eaten by monsters in a weekly session of Dungeons & Dragons with her trouble maker friends.

Robert Savino

Lake Squalls

. . . for the Lady of the Lake (Ronkonkoma)

Indian Girl, Indian Girl,
so much is written of you,
insatiable legend of a lake,
overflowing with tears of reprisal.

Two black eyes hide the red rage
as you move among the dead,
crossing the silver path
in the quiet spill of moonlight.

I stand, lakeside, barefoot
on wet leaves, not to lament
but to challenge what so many
fear . . . that thirst of the deep.

Indian Girl, Indian Girl,
perhaps you're merely a myth
in the nethermost bowel
of a bottomless inkwell.

Robert Savino, Suffolk County Poet Laureate 2015-2017 and Bards Laureate 2019-2021 is a native Long Island poet, Board Member at the Walt Whitman Birthplace and Long Island Poetry & Literature Repository Center. Robert is co-editor of two bilingual collections of Italian Americans Poets, *No Distance Between Us.* His books include *fireballs of an illuminated scarecrow, Inside a Turtle Shell* and *I'm Not the Only One Here.*

Leslie Simon

Let Me Count the Ways

I love thee my dear Long Island
being smitten a lifetime ago
feeling soft breezes of the tides, dining delectable cuisines

never enough of culinary retreats by the sea,
a sanctuary for me where troubles translate into peace
an odyssey that started way before the crowds

my first stop always, the Lobster Inn
an early brunch of mussels
while watching the ducks paddle by, they stop for us to throw them
bread

lying on the sand at Hither Hills Beach, always a personal require-
ment
my emotional home to connect with the waves
and ask advice from the ocean

Gossmans, at the most eastern tip of Long Island stands one of my
favorite haunts indulging on clams and lobsters, treasures fishermen
haul off their ships.
from my seat at the restaurant, I watch them enter the harbor from
long days at sea

driving out east on the south fork has always been my scenic haven
to pass by shops, flower gardens, restaurants and world class pristine
beaches
my remedy for shedding worries and filling my soul with contentment

---

Leslie is an award winning author. Her poems have appeared in several anthologies and recently published, *Pieces of My Heart*. It tells the story of her journey from depression and loss, to healing and recovery. Her book is unique in that it is illustrated by her vibrant handmade quilts which evoke emotions of each poem.

Joseph Stanton

The Invisible Man at Grad School

He had an advantage at Hofstra—
no need to pay tuition.
Still, there were bad days.

He was always counted absent
and no amount of raising his hand
could let him ask a question

or argue a point.
Chairs were safe for him
only in empty rooms.

He could cruise
the dorms
and ogle beautiful women in dishabille,

but, when he'd wink and whistle,
they'd turn to the teapot.
Sadly,

he never completed his studies.
Distaining the "No Walk" sign
at a crosswalk at Front Street,

he darted across
and was run over by a truck.
The driver, of course, saw nothing.

The invisible man
remained an unseen
bump in the road for months.

Joseph Stanton's eighth book of poems is *Lifelines: Poems for Winslow Homer and Edward Hopper*. His poems have appeared in such journals as *Poetry*, *Harvard Review*, *New Letters*, *Antioch Review*, *New York Quarterly*, *Long Island Quarterly*, and *Poetrybay*, as well as in several Paumanok anthologies.

Douglas G. Swezey

Dispiritedness

The joke is George Washington, our country's father, was narcoleptic
Because he slept everywhere on the North Shore of Long Island
Which is where he took his first tour of a newly formed country
After democratically being elected its first president
Following the Spy Trail used throughout the Revolutionary War

To pass messages and documents back and forth under the
Noses of those cocky and unsuspecting Redcoats
Between patriots in the City, those out east and all
Stops in between, like the Peace and Plenty Inn of Huntington
Providing food, drink and comfort to travelers and townspeople

Where Eliphalet Chichester, owner of tavern and taproom, served
In the Suffolk County Militia, having signed in 1775, an oath to
defend by arms these United Colonies, supplying goods to rebels
By raiding Loyalists, holding entire town meetings in the only
House with the space necessary using a hinged wall that opens up

Eliphalet passed in 1811, but still roams the rooms of the
National Landmark, or possibly it's his despondent son, Asa, who
Closed the inn, visitors hearing the footsteps falling on the second
Floor of the 1662 dwelling, witnessed by the likes of Teddy and
Whitman, born just down the road, and stopped by for hog guessing

Lamps and candles vanishing, others having heard Asa's footsteps
And seeing his footprints lead from the house: guilt for having
Transformed Peace and Plenty to a private dwelling, driving him
From his nearby grave back to his old home
It's difficult to disappoint your parents.

Allison Teicher-Fahrbach

You Know What You Did

I never got a chance to say goodbye to what once was.

One moment, he sat there next to me in that darkened cafe, confessing his darkest dreams over a cup of coffee. You know those stories: The ones that start with "I have never told anyone this, but I feel comfortable with you."

And suddenly, an illusory sense of comfort makes you lean in, your head perched in your hand, your elbow digging further and further into the confines of the table separating the two of you. And your ears crave to hear the inner twistings of the human mind.

Those once-inner thoughts that dare emerge into the light of existence.

A chance that cannot be remiss, all constructed on the basis of a transparent sense of trust.

Of honesty.

The words spilling from his mouth utter the very words that give you the feeling of a car accident: You want to look away, yet there is something so pungent about the scent of chaos in the air.

So you stay.

You watch and listen to every blaring siren and red flag that whisks through the air.

You let the aroma of burning fumes embrace your soul.

And you stand there or sit there, holding every moment tenderly as it passes...

Because in some sick, twisted way, you are grateful that you are standing behind the yellow "Do Not Cross Line" tape... and not laying in a puddle of your own misery, watching your own life shift terribly as the sirens beat directly on your existence.

Yet bystanders are not totally innocent of the grimy intricacies that lurk through every peripheral corner of darkness.

As the rain poured from the sky, the neon letters glistening from the cafe's sign dragged me back to some semblance of reality.

The man before me morphed into a monstrous entity.

Something that Edgar Allan Poe or Mary Shelley would only dream of, yet resist creating this character with mere paper and pen for its very existence is proof that evil can permeate even the most gentle of minds.

Humanity may be inherently good-natured, though this being before me somehow managed to ensnare my soul in a cage of tattered promises and alluring hope that another person can alter an individual's trauma without his active consent.

'This cannot be real,' I muttered under my breath. 'This is just a passing moment.'

Yet he continued to speak.

Yet he continued to kill with only his words as a weapon.

While nursing a steaming cup of coffee between my fragile fingertips, I felt my chest sinking deeper into a state of despair.

The thunder and lightning were bickering outside the window, and I wondered exactly how they decided who went first.

Why did each of their exchanges involve shock and suspense?

We see a flash of lightning, then cower under the ferocious boom of the thunder.

We see the ones we thought we knew changing before our eyes, then we hear the roar of their discrepancies.

My eyes must have been drifting from our conversation, for it did not feel the same as he called my name. The letters that formed my very being sounded like the hissing of a snake when he spoke my name.

His presence slithered and shifted before my eyes, but all I could hear was the hissing of his tongue slurping up a coffee between the hatred he was expressing.

Everyone and everything in his past was against him.

Everyone that he once loved wronged him, and he had no responsibility in the matter.

Everything was gray, for it would be contrastive in nature if it were black and white. It would all make sense if it were black and white, as there would just be two sides. Though his stories were laced with what he deemed to be "honesty" and "trust," the truth seemed to lack a sense of reality.

The ultimate horror of it all imbues your soul: Once you hear or see something, it cannot be erased.

It cannot be unheard.

It cannot be unseen.

We are left with remnants of a life once lived without this information.

In the next second, it was as if he evaporated into thin air. The scent of his cologne still lingered somewhere under my nose, though the man before me was nothing like what he initially seemed to be.

He became the mysterious figure behind each missing poster hanging on the wall, the victims only to be discovered with the passing of time, not the realization of the being behind their pain.

I am sure they all trusted him as well, or at least to some extent.

In hindsight, I wish I had never absorbed the agonizing words that spilled from his very lips.

Had I known what he was going to do–

Had I known that the words he was sharing would be taking a life–
Had I known what he was capable of... I am unsure I would have
positioned myself as a purveyor of innate curiosities. I may have still
sat there, gazing out the window, watching the raindrops fall to the
floor with a passionate fervor.

And my coffee may have tasted more of a delicate Brazilian rainforest
thousands of miles away from his crimes.

I would be safe from the horrors of his crimes, but I would never
escape the reality that I was complicit in his actions... even for a short
time.

The claws of a killer dig deeper into the hearts of those who never
realize that the care being shown was not reciprocated.

It never could be.

People can only care or be compassionate to the level of their own
self-love.

When we cling too much to the ghosts of what could have been, what
should have been, and what would have been, our fingers slip through
the sands of time.

You may always be grasping at what you think is in front of you still,
yet it is long gone.

Some may even wonder if it was meant to be there in the first place.

Still, we become a part of the ghost story. You become the villain in
a person's story when you see the previously unseen, hear the previ-
ously unheard, and actualize the reality that sitting across from an-
other being in a cafe is both the beginning and end of what once was.

Do we ever realize how our stories influence the invisible audience
around us?

Do we think about who we are creating in the process of creating
ourselves?

I think, above all, that is the biggest horror of them all.

As he sat there, continuing to pour his thoughts from his mind with the tenacity of five-days-past-the-expiration-date milk, I began to notice how each of the ghosts would embrace me.

It was as if they knew me.

They held me just as I held them: In a higher regard than he ever could have seen them in.

I could see the outline of their faces.

I could feel their names dance across my heart.

Even if he claims to have buried them long ago, I still think about them.

It revives them.

It brings them back to life.

Once we frame those who we consider to have wronged us as "ghosts," they do not disappear forever.

They will haunt you as long as you try to erase their ghosts, for you can hide all you want, but you cannot erase their souls.

Ghosts can walk through walls.

They will move into each layer of your lifetime.

"Why they did this to me, I will never know–"

The steam from the coffee cups before us had evaporated as quickly as his words.

"It's just not fair," the tears began streaming down his face.

So we sat there, the ghosts surrounding us, with his words waiting to sting my soul–

We remained silent, with the rain as the only audible soundtrack between the two of us.

Yet the ghosts were there.

They always were, and they always would be.

Had I known what he was going to do–

Had I known that the words he was sharing would be taking a life–

Had I known what he was capable of–

I would have heard the words the ghosts were whispering in our ears: "I may be invisible, but I will never disappear…"

Allison Teicher-Fahrbach is an educational leader who is passionate about the fields of somatics and multilingualism. Her fifth book, *Darkness, to Light,* was published in 2023. She is working on a number of different education-related projects and plans to defend her doctoral dissertation about trauma-informed education in late 2023.

James Tucker

There is no school on School Street

No child, the walk wasn't too long
Nor was it uphill both ways
But there was a little hill
To sled on snowy days

That's how I went to my old school house
But we can't go there now
In my mind it has to stay
It has disappeared somehow

To see it then you'd be so sure
It would stand the test of time
As mighty as the giant oak
In its courtyard we would climb

That courtyard had a flagpole too
And some lucky dog would raise
The stars bars Red White and Blue
Gallantly in Autumn set ablaze

How it waved through peace and wars
Over school yard battles too
While Tin soldiers settled scores
The girls had better things to do

Against its wall we hit the ball
A thousand times or more
No stadium had better claim
In Baldwin town folklore

Then in one summer slumber
I looked up from our porch
And saw machines lurch and lumber
In the sunlights dying torch

In my disbelief I rubbed my eyes
And just like that... It was gone
I called out in whispered cries
Rob Chris Dan Joe and John

How can bricks just vanish
Where did the Oak and flagpole go
Don't dwell upon it brother
There's more important things to know

And they all lay up ahead of you
So keep your eyes open wide
Someday new things will appear
For a little one walking by your side

James Tucker is a retired FDNY firefighter. Values time with loving family and friends. Enjoys reading and writing poetry among other things.

John Jay Tucker

Trouble Brewen

He prays for God
To end his strife
Once piercing eyes
His vision clouds

A forsaken man
Who lost his wife
Her ruffian nameless
Never found

Amidst this shroud
Of darkness
Awakens a sleepy
Long Island town

He dwells
On the higher ground
Their home gone
To rack and ruin

Near a lake
Where she was drown
Folks hail him
Trouble Brewen

Her death
A subdued mystery
The sheriffs first
Unsolved crime

The couple's
Sordid history
Reared a preacher son
Their joy sublime

On Sundays
He attends mass
Never first
Inside the church

He feels better
Seated last
A bit unkempt
His boots track dirt

The service starts
With a holy hymn
As the reverend
Surveys his flock

His eyes settle
On next of kin
A tear born
The organist stops

The lector requests
All to stand
Holding their
Revered prayer books

This house of God
It's beauty claimed
Was built by
His powerful hands

And until this day
Studied by
The unrelenting lawman's
Harried look

John Jay Tucker is a grandfather residing in Nassau County Long Island who enjoys family, attending poetry events, daily walks and substitute teaching at Lawrence Woodmere Academy. Published poems in PPA literary reviews and Bards anthologies.

J R Turek

Conklin House Haunting

On the National Registry of Historic places,
built in 1750 by David Conklin, and occupied
by the Conklin family until 1911, it's one of
the first museums on Long Island. I had heard
from several people that the home was haunted
by a malicious spirit, spiteful specter who turned
off lights and locked doors. Curiosity drove me
to tour the house.

David Conklin was held prisoner by the British
in 1777, his wife and children stayed put there
in the farmhouse, the same white house where
George Washington visited on his 1790 tour
of Long Island. I saw the table and chair where
he sat he sat in this history-rich 2.5 storied gabled
home located at the present corner of High Street
and New York Avenue in Huntington, New York.

No ghosts greeted us this Sunday afternoon;
a friend and I moved from room to room viewing
artifacts and hearing revolutionary facts, like
Sleep tight and don't let the bed bugs bite
originating from bedframes held together with ropes
that needed frequent tightening, and from mattresses

filled with rushes swept up and generally containing
bugs. Moving through periods of time where
the house reflected Colonial, Federal, and Victorian
period furnishings, I expected but was disappointed
when several fashionably dressed ghosts failed to
welcome us.

Our docent, wise and informative, took us upstairs
to see the first house on Long Island to have closets.
Yes, a perfect place for ghosts to hang around but no,
nothing but two tiny closets set with a fireplace
between them. Dangerous, I thought when a crash
behind us made our docent gasp, hand on her chest,
eyes wide with fright.

Behind us, about ten or twelve feet away
was the only furniture in the room. An armoire with
tall doors and wide drawers below. The doors had
flung open wide, banging against their piano hinges.
Odd indeed. No one there, we three on the other side
of the room and yet the doors continued to bang open
shut open shut.

Braver than I felt, I approached the armoire, steering
clear of the swinging wood doors. And then, they
stopped. I could hear the docent breathing heavy, still
standing beside the fireplace, my friend beside her.

I looked in, saw three shelves lined up with shoes.
Yes, shoes; moccasins, children, adult, beaded, plain
all shoes glorious shoes. I laughed and kept laughing

until the two women came up behind me, curiosity propelling them.

"Shoes," I said. "Neat rows of shoes, some with purple beads."

The docent gasped something unintelligible, hands on the doors to close them but they would not stay shut. She pulled some paper from her pocket, rolled it up and wedged it under the door, but still, they swung open. My friend, laughing and sputtering, told me to go in the hall, that the doors would never close if I stayed. I took another loving look at the collection, went into the hall and the doors were closed and stayed closed.

The remainder of the house tour, shortened I am sure by the uninvited ghostworks, was uneventful. We chuckled all the way home, referencing my attraction to shoes, and the poor docent who had probably never experienced anything like that day. My extraordinary shoe collection surpassed 500 pair yet the ghost wanted me to see what I didn't have. A mischievous encounter I embrace, one that fills me still with appreciative laughter.

J R (Judy) Turek, Superintendent of Poetry for the LI Fair, 2020 Hometown Hero, 2019 LI Poet of the Year, Bards Laureate 2013-2015, editor, mentor, workshop leader, and author of seven poetry books, the most recent *DogSpeak* is supporting North Shore Animal League, the *world's* largest no-kill shelter. 'The Purple Poet' has written a poem a day for 19 years; she lives on Long Island with her soul-mate husband, Paul, her dogs, and her extraordinarily extensive shoe collection. msjevus@optonline.net

71

Rekha Valliappan

Ghost in the Pines

About forty years ago on a date late in September a train drew up at Quogue a small station in Eastern Long Island. Out of it stepped a young man carrying a briefcase and some papers tied in a packet. The station was hardly crowded, although for this time of year past the summer it was usually sparse. He was expecting to be met from the way he looked around.

"Miss Adele!" at last he called out having spotted whom he wanted. Soon the two were shaking hands warmly.

"So you do know this part of the country," said Ms. Adele after a short interval.

"Why yes indeed! This vast expanse of wetlands and pitch pine trees was the subject of my entire plant phytology reaearch."

"I must admit, I don't know a nicer part of the island, my favorite haunt, as I call it," spoke Ms. Adele excitedly, as if agreeing mentally to a puzzle.

"Oh, it is a pleasant part really—except--that poor woman's sudden death--"

Ms. Adele looked suitably flustered, but only for a moment, as she searched for her frilly handkerchief "Oh dear, how dreadful of me to forget! Did she suffer from any

special illness for her age?" She knew this to be unlikely since it did not come out at the inquest, but felt it polite to ask.

"None that I know. However, that oddly proportioned Lodge near the towering tree at the south entrance to the Preserves does have a looming presence. It's all here just as I promised," replied the young botanist handing over the papers in the packet, then hurrying off, just as suddenly as he had come.

At the risk of sounding rather foolish after the site obtained legendary renown which needs no introduction, the place on the outskirts of the historic village of Quogue the plant expert found himself was The Pine Barrens. It is not very different from what it used to be. Marshes one end intersected by bogs overgrown with reeds and gorse inland, recalling the many chapters of Frankenstein, large duck pond to the west merging with the old schoolhouse grounds, fir woods forming a dark line, a long sea front yellow with sand dunes, and a quaint street to the east. How well I remember the trudge up a small muddy incline. No cottages as you turn the road except wind-beaten old pitch pines, strong winds, bright green grass which slowly vanish the further you reach, and blue sea

in the summer. My favorite "haunt" since it keeps its place in my affection. Any contrary tales that I hear of is of interest to me.

One such tale came to me in a place not too far from this spot, quite by accident, from a chance encounter with a herbalist Professor of

Botany from the University of Pennsylvania whom I had not met in years. I used to go to East Quogue fairly frequently.

I was happy there with my view of nature. Since the tale I haven't cared to go there anymore. It's intangible, but I don't know if I should venture once more into the pine forest, not after the curious series of troubling events that occurred which he told me of.

It was in mid-October several decades ago the woman was first sighted. Either lost or stranded by some chance she was the only person that night along the Old Country Road veering into the Pine Barrens. She stumbled upon a remote lodging house, practically empty. It was the Pine Lodge. Everyone who has traveled over Long Island for the better part of a century knows the haunted dwellings with which it is studded.

Dotted with the remains of old carriage roads and historical remnants dating back to the early 1800s there are quite literally ghostly farmhouses, cemeteries, ruins and more within the entire expanse, not forgetting the windmill, the lighthouse, the psychiatric asylum, the house of horrors, even a lake, usually surrounded by park-like greenery.

Remains of rustic seats, an old corrugated oak post somewhere near in faded letters, declaring what reads "You Are Entering Core Pine Barrens", gives rise to the ominous conjecture that a plantation or estate having fallen into neglect may have once stood there. Makes your hair stand on end, since there were marks and scratches on the old post, but one can't be sure.

For me it has always been the woods which had a very strong attraction, the line of dark pitch pines and scarlet oaks, the insect-catchers and rare orchids. Then I liked the eighteenth century feel of the Gothic structures, red brick or stone, some Italianate covered in marble, the great hall inside, the grain of the timber, the balustrades, insulated

from the outside. I think, not after the Great Fire that stunted the trees could the Old Pine Barrens return. Still, I believe much has been done by way of restoration of the whole to keep these preserves together. But the one feature that marks out the approach from a string of others, for the purpose of my tale, is gone. As you look at the view from the South Country Road that merges with the Old Country Road you will notice the point of intersection to a muddy lane the woman had taken, where you would have seen a grand old pitch pine over sixty feet high which had reached its full dimensions of twenty inches diameter in its 150 years lifetime. It had stood in the midst of a few dozen cedars and oaks.

The pines contributed a victim. On dark cold nights it is particularly nightmarish to contemplate, I'm told. As revealed the story came to me from my chance encounter with my botanist friend whom I will call Prof. McKeen for the purposes of this story. I needn't spend time describing him. The main thing is he is a plants specialist whom I got to know rather well. What I learned from him was first hand. The rich otherworldly history of Long Island's 'haunts' placed a young woman at the full harvest moon gathering pine cones from the droppings off the gigantic old pitch pine at the corner of the road. She had earlier wandered to the bog and was cutting off bladderworts with a sharp carving knife, muttering two-syllabic mantras to herself or so it seemed when a couple of botanists at work on insectivorous sundews and flesh-eating pitcher plants spotted her. She took alarm and sped off like a hare running across a garden.

On the third day it was a drizzly windy October morning. The two botanists, my friend and his partner, persuaded to take the same path as the woman, encouraged by what they expected to find in the way of carnivorous plant species were struck by what they saw. They were in plain sight of the large pitch pine. They saw a moving looking creature running up and down the thick plated trunk of the pine. But in the semi light of the cloudy day they could not make out the creature or its color. The sharp outline seen for barely a few seconds however was imprinted on their minds. They could have sworn though on hindsight it may sound foolish that racoon or not the creature definitely had more than four legs.

Next day the young woman was not downstairs at six in the morning at the Pine Lodge as was her practice. When several hours passed with no sign of her, two maids were sent to knock at her chamber door. Nothing. The door was opened at last from the outside and they found the young woman inside. She was dead and gray. There were no visible marks of violence, but the window was open. The coroner was immediately sent for. An inquest could not reveal the least trace of forced entry. A brew of half-emptied apple cider lay on the side table, visibly untouched. The drink was carefully examined but nothing of a venomous nature seemed present in it. Still, poison was the talk of the town on account of the swelling and grayness of the corpse. The face was nothing that Prof. McKeen had ever seen, stilled in the rigor mortis of extreme agony. The first maid who was one of those assigned to dress the corpse and prepare her for burial developed a vague shaking of the limbs which did not leave her till the day of her death.

Upon hearing of this sudden malady to afflict those who came into contact with the dead woman, my botanist friend took the maid immediately to a local physician for a careful examination of her hands and the skin of her palms which had most come in contact with the corpse. The doctor could not detect anything beyond a couple of small pin pricks which he concluded were the spots by which the poison was introduced. Prof.

McKeen remembered the stiff pine needles. His partner recalled the sticky tentacle sundews both thread-leaved and spatulate-leaved prickly specimens the young woman was foraging among the pines.

Thereafter the two botanists parted company, their work at an end, one to his Rhode Island abode, my friend the professor to his research station in Pennsylvania.

Likely to never meet again, the findings of which was not recorded for three score years.

So ends this first part of the Pine Barrens mysterious tragedy. It is to be mentioned that the room in which the young woman died was boarded up and never occupied. Nor was it slept in by anyone. Those who are interested in the statistical history of The Pine Lodge will find documented details in The Long Island Botanical Society Newsletters of the '80s which draws facts from The Suffolk County Gazette of the 50s and the Horticultural Society's History of Rare Orchids, several hybrids of which were known to exist in the pre-fire Pine Barrens at the time. Needless to add the local pineys spent many a night quite unproductive I'm afraid in dwelling on all manner of clues on what they called 'the Pine Barrens sickness.'

For me the incident revived for a time stories and exploits of witches and the occult among early descendents of European settlers, dormant for over two hundred years or longer, although my much admired 'haunt' of Quogue stayed as engaging to me as ever, nervous as I was with Prof. McKeen's tale.

One morning a decade or so later my botanist friend happened to be back on Eastern Long Island, to hand over some important papers to a Ms. Adele. She had persuaded him to spend the night in Quogue. At first he was daunted but relented to her suggestion. They retired for the night to The Pine Lodge. Suddenly he awoke after a night of considerable discomfort. It had been windy and so cold his windows had rattled incessantly. But he had heard a scream. Although driven to return to the same lodge he was aghast at Ms. Adele's insistence for a room with a view. Her wish for reasons unknown was to see the gigantic old pine tree from her bedroom window, which could only be possible from the shuttered chamber. The lodge keeper had been at the end of his wits.

"But why oh why did you let her demand for the locked chamber?" I asked in horror.

"Well just for one night" said she in pleading passion. Such is the lure of 'haunts.'

After which she had hurried off.

"But no one has slept there in ten years! A young woman died there," had remonstrated Prof. McKeen, besides himself.

"What use are these notes you gave me? Let me look at the chamber at least. I must see that tree."

There was no denying her. So the room was opened and indeed the musty smell was dank and earthy with a great foulness. Ms. Adele crossed to the window and impatiently threw open the shutters. As was expected and otherwise concealed from view, the great pine tree shook into focus. There was very little light, but in the half-darkness a shape clad in gray stood near her silhouette enshrouded in hairy tendrils. It seemed to emerge out of the tree's long shadow effortlessly. Two or three screams followed, all from Ms. Adele. Prof. McKeen was in a semi-faint unable to move.

"Cut it down! Cut it down!" Ms. Adele screamed in severe distress.

"Rest assured we can do no such thing, not to an ancient relic of the Preserves, who survived the great fire," cried out the innkeeper distraught, jumping up in fright and running out of the room.

Obviously country folk hold onto all manner of superstitions for generations.

Prof. McKeen made it clear to me he was a convinced disbeliever of the supernatural.

"You mean you don't at all believe in ghosts or sudden creatures or anything of the kind?" I asked with some trepidation in my voice, for generally I'm a firm believer of what local people believe. After cautiously inquiring about local traditions surrounding witchcraft and 'hauntings' McKeen a great world traveler of foreign towns who fell upon the subject of his research as a connoisseur of Byzantine coins or rare medieval manuscripts might, took me in confidence that he had seen a very similar occurrence in India. The compromised tree in that incident was the banyan tree.

Within hours the local pineys were demanding to know why in her condition Ms. Adele was allowed to open the forbidden room and view the pine tree. The air in the room could drive anyone to insanity they said. They agreed the scratches on the window pane must have been rats. The first day thus passed quietly and night came. And now Ms. Adele is in the room with the lights out. The outside is cold and windy. The window stands open. There is a piercing scream. There is very little light about the bed, but there is a strange movement there. It seems as if her body is all head and her hands are rotating rapidly to and fro. And now you can guess so deceptive is the darkness that she has several oversized hands round and grayish and several man-sized feet which move back and forward. It is a horrible illusion. There! Something charges off the bed and is out of the window in a flash—another—another—eight--after that there is quiet again. Some old folks will later say they see a ghost's footmark, a horribly thin corpse-like woman sitting on the window sill.

I dare say it was, someone or something creature-like on all fours, with not a sound except the wind. The subject of a real ghost has never been more uppermost in my mind. I imagine seeing strange crawling gray figures since.

As with the first tale of The Pine Lodge, so it was with Ms. Adele— gray and swollen and dead in bed.

An inquest finds no struggle, just a mound of gray dust in the dead woman's mouth and on her head, but the real cause of death is heart failure. The farmhands search the tree, the fork in the boughs where the gray creature has emerged, the marks gnawed in the trunk. Suddenly there is a petrified yell. Slithering down the sides of the tree is a man-sized creature taking fright.

"I always felt there were dim presences waiting for us near the tree," recounted McKeen, more in a dead faint than I had ever seen him. "There was nothing to be seen in front of the lodge except a line of dark dwarf pines which the fire had destroyed and were set to regrow. Yet in all the quiet a restrained hostility festered, like the trees were dogs on a leash just waiting to snap."

The gardeners pull out shovels and are busy in no time shoveling the soil around the roots of the tree. "The notion that we have is to dig for something which will fill us with dread. You can imagine how we wondered what face it would show, and what the end for us would be. Such dismal and horrid thoughts coursed through our minds." You could only tell in time the top soil was dug and a deep hole was created.

"We bent over shining our flashlights into the dark hole. That was enough. As if from a distance a voice seemed to say 'You have penetrated into the heart of the mystery, unaided.'" I'm estimating it was a matter of eighty years since anyone had seen these roots. But what Prof. McKeen saw that day made him recoil and throw himself back with a convulsion of despair.

His botanist partner was there at the bottom, a skeleton of a woman besides who took shape as a burnt human form. You don't need to be told that both were clean dead for a very long time. Her mouth was full of sand and pine cones. His teeth and jaws were broken. Just as the others were clambering to get to the bodies, no one reveals any knowledge of the woman, or of any missing woman or women in these parts. It came upon me that the grey thing or things were creatures of darkness which our minds induce and that they could not move in the daylight.

I've often asked the older pineys in the village whether they knew of anything strange, but either they knew nothing or they wouldn't tell me. Needless to add the trees, the post and the Lodge were never cleared. New innkeepers took over the building, covered it in stucco, renaming it The Red Lion after one Mandarin New Year on which the sale of The Pine Lodge was executed.

As I have opined when I chose to tell this tale, something draws one to a 'haunt.'

And I have never been at the Pine Lodge, or even near it, since.

The End

Rekha Valliappan is a multi-genre writer of short stories and poetry. Her writing has featured in various literary and genre journals including The Museum of Americana: A Literary review, Wings of Wonder: A Poetry Anthology, StepAway Magazine's 'Imaginarium' Fantasy Issue, Litro Magazine, Adelaide Literary Magazine, Ann Arbor Review, Utopia Magazine of Science Fiction, and elsewhere. She has won awards for her writing and earned nominations for the Pushcart Prize and Best of the Net.

James P. Wagner (Ishwa)

Long Island Haunts Me

Amityville Horror...
The Princess of Lake Ronkonkoma...
Kings Park Pilgrim State Psychiatric Center...
Just a few off the Long Island Haunts
That have captured the frightened minds
Of so many from so many places...
And like so many others,
Long Island Haunts me...
But not the same way.

I was born here,
I grew up here...
I have lived here my entire life
And everywhere I look
I see ghosts.

Not those ghosts...
Other ghosts...
Familiar ghosts...

I am haunted by the playgrounds
Where my Grandma used to take me to
When I was a child
I am haunted by the streets, near my parents house,
Where I used to bike up the roads to see friends

In every direction.
I am haunted by the building that used to be my Dad's hobby shop
Where I had my first job
In what seems like a different lifetime...
I am haunted by the big grassy field
That I used to go to with my friends
On Fridays, after High School
And the restaurant we used to eat at
That is no longer there.

I am haunted, by the old mansion
In disrepair
In Oakdale, where I went to college
Met my wife,
And had so many happy memories...

I am haunted by the faces,
Of friends, and family
Who have passed on...
Who used to make this area bright and sunny.

I am haunted by the many who have chosen
To move on from this place
To other callings...
I am haunted by the images,
And phantoms...
Of what was,
and will never be again.
And I,
like a ghost,
an entity who has clung to a place...

long past the time that they belonged...
Continue to haunt Long Island,
As it haunts me.

Jillian Wagner

The Tale of the Stormy Night

I actually enjoy a night in when there's a storm outside and I never really liked school parties. But when you're alone during a storm, there's no telling what could happen, is there?

Lily shuddered as thunder boomed above her. The thunder was followed by a shriek of wind that made the car windows rattle. Lily bit her lip, eyes focused on the headlights illuminating the road before her. She hoped she could make it home before the storm hit. Lily could tell the weather was going to be bad tonight and was grateful she would be staying in.

The trees lining the road were naked, the last of the autumn leaves having fallen days ago. Their bare branches, skeletal fingers in the darkening evening, seemed to reach out for her as she turned onto her street. The wind moaned again, making the branches sway and creak ominously overhead, but Lily paid them no mind. She was almost home and eager to be inside her warm, comfortable house.

By the time Lily pulled into her gravel driveway, the first drops of rain had begun to fall. Grabbing her backpack, bag of Taco Bell, and large cup of soda, the seventeen-year-old made a beeline for the house. Yanking the door open, Lily darted inside and locked the door as the rain began to fall in earnest. Breathing a sigh of relief, Lily flicked on the hall light and the living room was flooded with a warm glow. From the couch, a mound of black and white fur stirred and blinked at her.

"Hi, Jet," Lily called as the cat came over to rub against her legs. "Did Mom forget to feed you again?" Jet meowed pitifully as Lily walked into the kitchen. His gaze followed her as Lily set her tacos on a plate and shoved it into the microwave.

"I think I can give you something in the twenty seconds it takes for my tacos to heat up." Lily hit the microwave button, then retrieved Jet's dish. From the cupboard under the microwave, Lily snagged a can of cat food and dumped it into Jet's green dish. She had just set the cat's food down when the microwave beeped.

"Perfect timing."

Jet watched as his mistress washed her hands, but ignored her and began eating as Lily grabbed her own dinner and carried it into the living room. She turned on the electric fireplace and flopped down onto the puffy sofa. Slipping off her shoes, Lily pulled the coffee table closer; as she did, she noticed her new book (a real-life case study on well-known serial killers) had been set there. Picking it up, Lily noticed something else had been left for her: a note.

Lily,

This arrived today. I hope, though, that you changed your mind and are going to the dance. You have a life-time to read, but you'll only be young once. You need to have a social life.

Love,

Mom

Lily snorted with impatience before crumpling the paper and tossing it to the floor. Let Jet play with her mom's wishes; Lily was just grateful that her parents were out tonight themselves. With her mom and dad at a company gala and her sister at college (and probably partying herself), Lily could have some peace.

Propping her book on her lap, Lily bit into her first soft taco. The steaming hot beef, warm lettuce, and melted cheese, all wrapped up in a flour tortilla, reminded her of how hungry the last half of the day had made her. Lily forced herself to eat slowly and sip her Mountain Dew rather than gulp. God, between running a six-minute mile in P.E. (her last period) and getting a head start on her homework, Lily hadn't had a chance to eat since noon. Oh, well, it was worth it.

"Head start nothing, Jet," Lily said as the cat returned to the living room. "Finished my English essay, all my math, and turned in my history project early. Now my weekend's free and my college applications are done too. I'm betting the kids partying tonight will be begging for a project extension on Monday."

Jet purred and licked a paw, the fire's flames flickering in his green eyes.

"Right," Lily agreed, finishing her fourth taco. "And I'm pathetic for *not* going to the stupid fall dance."

Almost on cue, Lily's cell phone vibrated. Sipping more Mountain Dew, Lily reached into her pocket and pulled out her phone. The screen was alight with a question.

Where U at? Lily sighed.

At home with Jet. Roughly two seconds later, another message popped up.

Ur not cumming?

No, Chelsea, I'm having dinner. Lily could almost hear her friend's trademark whine in the next message.

But I thought u wuld cum. Jason's here. Not even wanting to touch the innuendo, Lily typed,

Isn't Jason with Brittney?

No. They broke up yesterday. Brittney's w/ Derek now. Y aren't U cumming? Ur mom said u wuld.

My mom says a lot of things. I didn't feel like going out on such a crappy night. If anything, the pounding rain and shrieking wind had picked up outside, making her statement all the more true.

Lily picked up her fifth and last taco; seriously, who actually *wanted* to be out on a night like this?

Apparently Chelsea did and she wasn't the only one. As she chewed the last bit of taco, Lily's phone buzzed yet again.

I want to see you.

Oh, great. Lily furiously typed her reply, mentally cursing Chelsea for giving out her number without her permission.

For the last time, Jason, my answer is no. Lily had no interest in being the senior stud's latest conquest. Love 'em and leave 'em was Jason's style, though he and Brittney had managed to remain a couple for quite some time. Likely, though, one of them had gotten bored with the other. Lily hoped she could leave some of this crap behind after high school.

Finishing her taco, Lily sat sipping the last of her Mountain Dew. Picking up her book, Lily flipped to the chapter on Albert Fish, sighing with contentment as her full stomach settled and the fire's heat caressed her chilled skin. Even then rain pounding overhead lent itself to the cozy atmosphere and Lily felt her whole body relax as she spent a cozy hour reading by the fire's light.

"This is a breaking news bulletin!" Lily jumped and whipped her head in the direction of the TV a few feet away. The screen displayed the local news station, the two news anchors ruffling documents on their desks. On the loveseat opposite the couch was Jet, his paw still on the remote.

"Again, Jet?" Lily asked with a relieved grin. "Geez, one of these days, you're gonna give me a heart attack."

Lily retrieved the remote from her purring pet, then turned back to the TV. One of the anchors, a woman with dark hair and green eyes, looked a little uneasy.

"Flash flood and mudslide warnings are in effect. Winds are going to be heavy, so watch for falling tree branches. The rain is predicted to continue until around 1:00 a.m. tomorrow morning. Temperatures are expected to drop down into the 20s at that time as well, turning the rain to ice. If you plan to drive tonight, please be careful."

"And this just in," her partner, an older man, chimed in. "We have just received word that a man by the name of Daniel Flemming has just escaped from police custody. Flemming was convicted of the torture and killing of five teenage girls. It is unknown if he is armed, but he is considered to be extremely dangerous. People are advised to keep their doors and windows locked. Please contact your local law enforcement with any information concerning Flemming's whereabouts."

Lily shut off the TV and turned on the light. Padding over to the front door, Lily double-checked the latch and was satisfied it was securely locked. Jet's eyes followed her as she checked the windows and then sat back down with a relieved sigh.

"All good. And we don't have a drain pipe or anything, so I can't see anyone climbing up to my room. I think we're safe, Jet." Jet meowed and twitched his tail. Lily looked at her cat and then at her book.

"Yeah, you're probably right. No more of this for tonight. Not with Daniel Flemming on the loose."

Lily shuddered. One of her elective classes last year had been Legal Studies and they had all followed the case of Daniel Flemming. Apparently, the man had worked as a janitor at a community center in the next county and was, as per his employers, a quiet loner. Yet, he had managed to abduct five young girls,- two from their homes, three from the center- overpower them and take them to his house. When police had uncovered the bodies (buried in his backyard; the smell had caused his neighbors to call the authorities in the first place), all of them bore marks of horrible torture. None of them had died easily.

"Now, what can we say about this case?" Mr. Peters, the teacher, had asked.

"Serial killers shouldn't bury bodies in their backyards?" Jason, who had taken the class along with Lily, had called out. Everyone but Lily had laughed.

"Daniel Flemming wasn't a serial killer," she clarified. "Due to a different amount of time passing between each killing and the fact that Flemming broke his pattern based on how he abducted the victims *and* how he tortured each girl differently, Flemming's motive was simply opportunity. He saw something he wanted and he took it. What's more, all of the girls Flemming took were themselves different; different body types, different hair color, one of them was African American and one was Asian while Flemming was Caucasian. So no, Flemming is not, nor will he be labeled a serial killer."

"Very true, Lily. And, may I say, expertly stated." Mr. Peters had agreed, pacing the rows of students as he spoke. "Police noted that the victims were either shot, strangled, or stabbed. All of them were sexually assaulted, but the torture of each of the victims was different and their methods of death were inconsistent with a set pattern. Flemming was also quoted to have saying that he simply liked 'watching pretty things squirm.' More the mark of a sociopath than a serial killer."

"Of course, Flemming may have taken more victims," Lily added. "The police aren't sure at the moment."

"Ahh, been doing a bit of extra research?" Mr. Peters asked with a smile. Behind him, one of the girls mouthed the word "nerd" at Lily through her bubblegum lips. Lily ignored her as she answered,

"Yes, I have. According to the head detective on the case, the forensic teams only *found* five victims in Flemming's backyard, but there was no way he'd carried out the torture in his own home The kitchen was too clean and he didn't have a basement. There was also a lack of the various instruments of torture Flemming used on his victims."

"Meaning?" Jason asked, cocking an eyebrow at Lily and giving her what he no doubt considered his sexiest look. Rolling her eyes, Lily replied,

"*Meaning* Flemming most likely had a secondary location he took his victims to. Unfortunately, he hasn't divulged any information regarding an alternate location, but if he resorted to burying bodies in his backyard- way too risky- it may mean that his previous dumping ground is now either unavailable or too crowded. No new bodies have been discovered yet, so more likely it's the latter."

"Excellent, Lily. I think you've earned an extra five points toward your grade," Mr. Peters said, making a note in his attendance book. "No that you need them, of course," he added with a wink.

"Share them with me, Lily," Jason murmured at the back of Lily's neck, his breath warm and smelling of fried grease.

"You wish," Lily hissed back. Raising her voice, she announced to the class,

"Flemming may be holding out the location of a secondary location and other victims in exchange for a plea deal. We'll know more as he's brought to trial."

"Indeed we will. And I encourage all of you to follow the trial," Mr. Peters told the class. "I'll give you extra credit points if you keep a log of the witnesses and statements, particularly Fleming's statement."

Unfortunately, Flemming had kept silent throughout most of the proceedings (except to cackle madly at the descriptions of the tortured girls). His refusal to cooperate on the stand and stubborn silences had earned him two consecutive life sentences, despite his lawyer's best attempts at swaying the jury to show some compassion.

"Please, that insanity defense wasn't going to work," Lily told Jet as she carried her garbage into the kitchen. "A *competent* lawyer should have been able to see that! Flemming was sane enough to know what he did was wrong, so said the police psychiatrist. Believe me, *I* did my research on that. Unlike *some* people."

A particularly violent shriek of wind caused more rain to lash against the windows. Lily shuddered as the tree branches rattled against each other like bones. Okay, this was just too much. Between the weather, the long day, and an escaped killer, Lily decided she would like nothing better than a hot bath and her warm bed.

"C'mon, Jet, let's go." Jet purred, but remained on the couch as Lily checked the door and windows one more time before turning out the lights. As she looked out the window, a flash of lightning illuminated the dark yard. Glancing out of the window, Lily thought she saw the silhouette of a man standing at the edge of the driveway. With a gasp, Lily flicked the main lights back on. Shaking a little, Lily looked back outside. Nothing; no one was there. Lily sighed and turned the lights back off.

"I'm losing my mind," she told Jett as she made her way upstairs. All the same, she'd lock the upstairs windows before she took her bath.

****

Oh, that felt good! Lily stretched out in the tub of bubble-topped steaming hot water, feeling the heat seep into the tired muscles of her legs and back. Ms. Vicks, the sour-faced gym teacher (who was no doubt chaperoning the dance tonight), must've known the track would be useless on Monday and wanted to make use of it while she could.

"Again, how anyone can dance after running a mile in the cold three hours ago?" Lily wondered aloud. "I mean, I did it in six minutes, but the other girls averaged about twelve and *they* complained the whole time." Outside the bathroom door, Jet meowed his agreement. Lily smiled, happy that her cat had developed the habit of waiting outside the bathroom for her to come out. The cat's contented meows were proof that she was safe in her warm house.

Lily sank into the lavender-scented bubbles, blocking out any thoughts of school dances and serial killers. Tonight, she'd dig out an old Disney movie or some other childhood cartoon and leave the horrors of reality for tomorrow. There'd be plenty of it too. And plenty of guilt on her mother's part, no doubt. Lily snorted; imagine trying to cajole her youngest daughter into going to a dance when there was an escaped killer on the loose!

"I would say that I would be safer among other people, but Flemming worked best in crowded settings," Lily informed Jet. "He just blended in and kept to himself, so unless you knew who he was, you ignored him. That's how he managed to kidnap those girls from the community center. And the girls he grabbed from their houses, he *followed* them. No way he would take a chance coming here."

Jet purred and Lily heard a soft dragging sound on the carpet, indicating that the cat had found one of his toys. She laughed and sank under the water, leaving only her nose poking through the bubbles. It was probably freezing outside; the wind chill could make November feel like January here on Long Island. Lily didn't envy her classmates, who were probably wearing less-than-ideal clothing. The girls especially seemed to wear summer fashions well into October! Ugh, no thanks!

Thump! Thump! Lily sat up, creating a mane of white froth around her face. What was that? Outside, Jet hissed once, but then went back to chewing on his toy. Lily shrugged; it might've been the gas generator taking over. The power could easily go out on a night like this. But did the generator kicking on usually sound like a fist pounding on a door?

No, no, she wasn't going to think like that! Lily reached for the shampoo bottle and began working the gel through her hair, forcing her thoughts to turn away from the possibility of someone outside. No one would want to be outside tonight!

"Besides, Jet," Lily said, "even if Daniel Flemming was nearby, why would he come here? I could be a cop for all he knows!"

Jet's friendly meow soothed the girl and she began to lather her body with a lavender-scented soap. No doubt Jason would've loved to catch a glimpse of her like this. He probably spent hours wondering what kind of soap she used, the pig!

Sccccrrreeeeetttcccchhhh!

Lily froze, the washcloth clenched in her hand. Was that a tree branch? Had a tree fallen over? She hadn't heard a crash. No, that sounded more like someone... dragging something sharp across a window. Jet must've thought so too because he scuttled away, no doubt to hide under her bed.

"Thanks, Jet, Lily muttered, pulling the plug on her bath. She was beginning to feel vulnerable, sitting here wet and naked. Time to get inside her safe bedroom with its latched window, thick drapes (for atmosphere, Lily had explained to her mom), and soon-to-be locked door.

Lily turned on the shower and quickly rinsed off. Grabbing her towel, Lily rubbed herself dry as fast as she could. She paused, then turned her hair dryer up to its highest setting so her short black hair would dry faster.

"It was probably just a tree branch. It was probably just a tree branch," she muttered over and over to herself as she brushed out her hair. "Just a tree branch. Of course it was." Come on, she wasn't one for flying off the handle. She could stay calm and think logically! Based on the wide eyes she saw in the mirror, though, she wasn't fooling herself.

Lily yanked on her flannel pajamas and slippers, wiped down the tub, and dumped her laundry into the hamper. Okay, good, chores were done. Now she could-

Riiiiinnnnggggg! The upstairs hall phone blared. Gulping, Lily carefully made her way down the darkened hallway and picked up the phone. She kept her eyes trained on her bedroom door, warm light spilling out from the crack Jet had made when he had retreated under her bed.

"Hello?" she asked. No one answered.

"Hello?" She thought she heard breathing.

"Who is this?" A heavy grunt.

"This isn't funny, Jason!" God, the idiot was trying to make an obscene call *now?* Was he really that horrible?

"You're disgusting!" A satisfied sigh and a click. Scowling, Lily checked the last number that had come through, expecting to see Jason's number. Instead, she recognized it as Chelsea's.

Fuming, Lily re-dialed. She heard Chelsea's phone ringing before it went to voice mail.

"Not funny, Chelsea! Why are you letting Jason use your phone anyway? He's just being a creep again!" Lily was about to hang up when she heard that same heavy breathing. Wait, *was* that Jason? It sounded... rougher.

"Yeah, tell Jason I said have fun. Bye!"

Lily dropped the phone back into its cradle. Immediately, it began ringing again, its shrill noise like nails on a chalkboard. Heart pounding, Lily raised the receiver back to her ear.

"Hello? Chelsea?"

"Lily, right?" a deep voice whispered.

Lily dropped the phone, not caring where it landed. She ran into her room, locked the door and pulled the curtains shut. She jumped into bed and yanked the covers over her head. For once, Lily wasn't thinking logically nor was she attempting to call the police. Daniel Fleming was out there and she wasn't moving from the safe little space in her room, no matter what!

****

Lily's eyes cracked open, focusing on the digital clock on her nightstand. The glowing red numbers read 9:25. Rubbing the sleep from her eyes, Lily sat up and pushed her comforter off her. From the edge of her bed, Jet stirred and glanced reproachfully up at her.

"Morning, Jet. I guess we both went a little crazy last night, huh?" Jet meowed happily and arched his back against Lily's hand as she scratched his ears.

"Yeah, I can't blame you. I was sure Flemming was trying to break into the house. Heh, talk about letting your imagination run away with you. I'm surprised I managed to fall asleep at all, but I guess I was so tired from yesterday that I was bound to in the end." Jet purred and rubbed his head against Lily's hand, his tail swishing over the blankets.

"I know," Lily agreed. "I expected to stay awake all night too. Like I said, my imagination ran away from me. But enough of that; I'll bet you're hungry, right?"

Jet meowed eagerly as Lily stood up, stretched and opened the curtains on her bedroom window. A cold fog obscured most of Lily's view of the yard and there was ice on the windowsill. The temperature must've dropped down to below freezing last night; unusual for November, but not unheard of. Lily shivered; maybe she'd have some hot chocolate with breakfast.

Eager to be downstairs, Lily made her bed and yanked on a pair of jeans and a thick sweater. Stopping off in the bathroom, she washed her face and brushed her teeth and hair before returning to the hall and replacing the phone back in its cradle. She had a feeling that the battery was in dire need of a recharge, but until then, she had her cell phone nestled in her back pocket.

"C'mon, Jet, let's go." The cat followed Lily downstairs, the living room walls pearly grey in the early morning sunlight. Lily glanced outside at the backyard; it was awash with frozen mud, the grass torn up from the storm. There were frozen leaves scattered about all over and several large branches, fallen from their trees, were buried in the muck.

"Huh, it really *was* a tree branch I heard," Lily said in relief. "And the news wasn't kidding about mudslides. Bet Mom and Dad stayed at a hotel last night." Lily decided to check the driveway just to be certain. Behind her, Jet jumped up onto the loveseat, watching her with interest. Slipping on her sneakers, Lily opened the front door, expecting to see her car alone in the driveway...

... and screamed.

A massive tree trunk had been split in half. One hunk of wood had toppled into a nearby cluster of trees. The other had fallen across the driveway, barely missing Lily's small car. But Lily found her eyes locked on a huddled shape buried under the wood and half-submerged in frozen mud. The crumpled figure's face was turned away from her, but one arm, encased in the sleeve of a dirty orange jumpsuit crusted with ice and mud, reached out toward the house. Clutched in that grimy hand was a serrated hunting knife, its blade shining in the frosty morning sunlight.

Head spinning, Lily raced back into the house, slammed the front door, and locked it tight. Fumbling for her cell phone, Lily's head jerked up as the TV blared to life.

"This just in!" Jet's green eyes stared at the TV, his paw still on the remote. "Seventeen-year-old Chelsea Peterson has been confirmed as missing by county police. Miss Peterson was attending a dance at her local high school last night when, friends say, she stepped out to make a call and never returned. Police are fearful that Daniel Flemming may be behind Chelsea's disappearance, but no evidence has yet been..."

Jillian D. Wagner currently resides in Northport, Long Island where she runs the Dog-Eared Bard's Book Shop along with her husband James. She has lived both in Amagansett on Long Island and Orange County in California, but a love of reading and writing has followed her no matter where she resided. She is a graduate of Dowling College and earned her paralegal certification from SUNY Binghamton. While she worked for a bank attorney for several years, Jillian is more than happy not just to work in a book store, but to share her writing with the world.

Margarette Wahl

History Haunts Us

History is supposed to haunt us.
Can you hear footsteps of Quaker settlers of the Bethpage Purchase?

History is supposed to haunt us.
Walk across grasses of Old Grace Church. The oldest church in Massapequa. Read the resting places of the Joneses. Learn how Jones Beach got it's name.

History is supposed to haunt us.
No one visits Raynham Hall,
9/11, or holocaust museums because they love all it marked
inside our timelines.

History is supposed to haunt us.
Slaves were light, red, tan, as dark as they were African skin.

History is supposed to haunt us.
Montauket, Merricks, Massapequas, Setaukets, Shinnecocks, Lenape.
With Cherokee flowing my veins,
Chief Standing Bear embraces
a postage stamp.The sachem of Long Island's history now
spark fierce debate
as town or school mascots.

History is supposed to haunt us.
This is how we learn it.
No one has a position
to eliminate anyone's past.
Society needs to remember
we can't erase ours.

Margarette Wahl is a Long Island Poet and Special Education Teacher Aide over twenty years. She's a member of Bards Initiative, Nassau County Poet Laureate Society, and Performance Poets Association. Her poems have been published in various anthologies and has four chapbooks with Local Gems Press.

Glenda Walker-Hobbs

Haunted House

the house stands in the middle
of a dark wood guarded by trees
with bare black branches,
the house is grey with peeling
paint and broken windows

a door hangs on its hinges,
as I enter it falls to the floor
with a deafening clatter,
the floor creaks as I travel across it,
a sudden crash and my foot
goes through the floor

ancestral portraits line the walls,
the eyes of grim-faced men
follow me as I move around the room,
a woman surrounded by flames
is being burnt at the stake,
is it possible she was a witch?

a dark object flies around my head,
bats circle the inside of the room
I duck, pray they will stay out of my hair,

as I back towards a wall,

something stringy falls across my face,
a spider has spun a web,
a ghost floats through the air,
moaning loudly and eerily

I panic,
scream like a banshee,
search for an exit,
burst out of the house,
scramble panting
to the nearest tree,
I pause,
turn around

only a giant black shadow remains

Glenda Walker-Hobbs is a Canadian poet and writer from Flin Flon
where she helped found a local Writers Guild and currently serves as
its secretary. She is a long-time member of Writers Village University
and co-moderator of Word Weavers Poetry Group as well as belong-
ing to an international poetry group that meets online. She has
achieved her Certificate in Creative Writing and is working on her
MFA in Poetry. She has published thirteen books of poetry, including
seven chapbooks with Local Gems Poetry Press and has had prose
and poetry published in various anthologies and e-zines including
Village Square.

Veronica Wulff

Bug Light

The eye illuminates the Peconic Bay
with slow, steady blinks,
telling men what to do in the dark
without words.

The lighthouse –
a beacon of hope, to some.
A giant bug at high tide,
to others.
To me, a symbol of God.

A wickie once lived inside its achy joints
and flooded the dim chambers
of its empty heart
with prayer and candlelight.

I am beckoned
to climb its spiral staircase.
Up a ladder by rope, I go
to the tippy top near heaven
where I can judge the world.

The balustrade cradles me
while the wind whistles

and the sea licks her lips,
watching and waiting
for ships to come by.

Veronica Wulff is a native New Yorker who was born and raised in Manhattan, lived in Queens, and is now a resident of beautiful Baldwin in Long Island. Veronica earned her Bachelor degree in Film Studies at Hunter College before kickstarting her 26-year long career as a producer of international adaptations of Sesame Street for kids all around the world. She enjoys reading autobiographies, writing poetry, watching reality tv, and cuddling with cats! When not at the beach with her significant other, you can find her exploring a new bookstore with her daughter, or sipping coffee on the porch.

About the Editor

James P. Wagner (Ishwa) is an editor, publisher, award-winning fiction writer, essayist, historian, actor, comedian, performance poet, and alum twice over (BA & MALS) of Dowling College. He is the publisher for Local Gems Poetry Press and the Senior Founder and President of the Bards Initiative. He is also the founder and Grand Laureate of Bards Against Hunger, a series of poetry readings and anthologies dedicated to gathering food for local pantries that operates in over a dozen states. His most recent individual collection of poetry is *Everyday Alchemy*. He was the Long Island, NY National Beat Poet Laureate from 2017-2019. He was the Walt Whitman Bicentennial Convention Chairman and has taught poetry workshops at the Walt Whitman Birthplace State Historic Site. James has edited over 100 poetry anthologies and hosted book launch events up and down the East Coast. He was named the National Beat Poet Laureate of the United States from 2020-2021. He is the owner/operator of The Dog-Eared Bard's Book Shop in East Northport, New York.

Made in the USA
Middletown, DE
09 October 2023

40389201R00066